The
Woodwinds

By JEAN CRAIG

Illustrated by GEORGE OVERLIE

Prepared under the supervision of Robert W. Surplus

Musical Books for Young People

LERNER PUBLICATIONS COMPANY
MINNEAPOLIS, MINNESOTA

ACKNOWLEDGEMENT

The publishers wish to express their appreciation to the Chester E. Groth Music Company, Minneapolis, for supplying many of the actual instruments illustrated in the text.

41372

CONTENTS

What Is a Woodwind?

Suppose someone asked you this question — what is a woodwind? First of all, you would probably name the five woodwind instruments — the *flute,* the *oboe,* the *bassoon,* the *clarinet,* and the *saxophone.* Then you could say that each of these instruments belongs to a family. This means, you could explain, that each of these instruments has one or more related instruments. A player of any woodwind can switch from his instrument to a related one quite easily. For instance, an oboe player can change to the English horn with almost no trouble at all.

But what about the word "woodwind"? What does it mean?

The second half of the word —"wind"— means that wood-winds are *wind* instruments — instruments made to sound by the breath of the player.

And what about the first half of the word? Are all woodwinds made of wood? No. The first woodwind instruments were made of wood. But today, the flute and saxophone are made of metal. Sometimes we even see metal clarinets. Many, less expensive clarinets, bassoons, and oboes are made of rubber.

Most people know that all brass instruments are made to play in the same way. They use a cup-shaped mouthpiece. The woodwind instruments, however, are not all made to sound in the same way. Most of them use reeds. The clarinet and saxophone use *single* reeds. The oboe and bassoon use *double* reeds. The flute doesn't use a reed at all.

Where can a person hear woodwind instruments played? Almost anywhere. Today, with the help of radio and television, it is easy to become acquainted with these instruments. All five wood-wind families can be seen and heard in any symphony orchestra or concert band. Besides these large performing groups, the woodwinds are also used in groups that play lighter music. The bassoon is the only woodwind that is not used in dance and jazz bands. Yes, even the flute now plays jazz!

There are many other questions that could be asked about the woodwinds. Where did these instruments come from? How are they made? Are they difficult to learn to play? How do they work? Let's take a closer look at each of the five families of woodwinds and learn the answers to these and other questions.

The Flute Family

Of all the wind instruments, the flute can do the most things the most easily. A fine performer on a flute can dash up a scale and down again so quickly that our ears cannot separate the notes. A flutist can skip and jump from note to note so lightly that the music reminds us of the quickness of a rabbit or of a gazelle. He can swoop and turn and trill the notes until we think that we are hearing a bird. Musicians say that a flute can do anything!

7

There is a funny story that shows this. A flutist and a friend were walking down the street one day. Pointing to a Chinese laundry, the friend asked the flutist if he could read the sign over the door. "No," said the musician, "but if I had my flute, I think I could play it."

A person seeing a flute for the first time with all its keys, might think that learning to play it must be terribly difficult. This is not so. Of course, like any musician, a flutist must practice for many hours and study for years before he can dash up and down a scale or sound like a bird. He is helped, however, by his instrument. Of all the woodwind instruments, the flute has the simplest fingering system. Let's take a look at a flute and see why it has been called the most perfect of the woodwind instruments.

What do we see when we look at a flute? It is a silver-colored instrument about twenty-six inches long. Most fine flutes in this country are made of silver. A few, very expensive flutes are made of gold or platinum. Today, the flutes of most beginners are made of stainless steel, because steel is less expensive than silver.

Once in a while, you may see a flute made of wood. A wooden flute has a softer, sweeter sound than one made of metal. All flutes used to be made of wood. Today metal flutes are used more than wooden flutes, because they can be played louder much more easily. A louder flute is needed so that it can be heard in our large, modern symphony orchestras and bands. It took a long time for the metal flute to take the place of the wooden flute. The great composer, Richard Wagner, would not allow metal flutes in his orchestra—he called them "cannons." Today, some people still prefer the sound of a wooden flute.

When we see a flute in its case, it is in three pieces, or *joints*. These parts are fitted one into another when the flute is put together. The names of the parts are easy to remember. They are the *head* joint, the *body* joint, and the *foot* joint.

The head joint is the part that is nearest the player's head. It has the *blowhole,* or *embouchure* (AHM-buh-shoor), on it. A flutist places the embouchure against his lower lip and blows a thin stream of air across the hole in order to make a sound. Have you ever sounded a note by blowing across the top of a soda pop bottle? Blowing a flute is very much the same.

The keys that are used to make the different notes on the flute are mostly on the body joint. There are three keys on the foot joint. When a flute player plays a flute, each finger works only one key, except for the left thumb and the right little finger.

Here is how the fingers are placed on a flute.

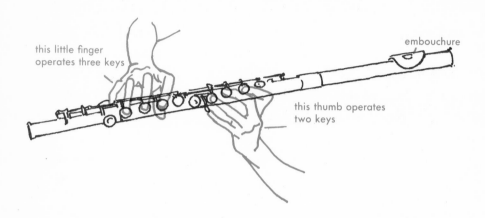

this little finger
operates three keys

embouchure

this thumb operates
two keys

Using just these keys, a flutist can play all the notes from
to . Some flutists can play even higher with
the use of special fingerings. A few flutes have a special foot joint
with an extra key. This special joint makes it possible to play
down to this note: .

How is it possible to play all these notes with just these
keys? To understand how this can be done, let's go back in his-
tory and look at some early flutes.

The flute is a very old instrument. As far as we know, people
in every part of the world have had flutes for thousands of years.
Flutes have been found in the homes of the ancient cave men.
You can see that through the years men must have made millions
of flutes. Yet every one of these flutes is sounded in one of only
two ways!

The first way of making a flute sound is by blowing across the blowhole, like you would blow across the top of a soda pop bottle. Flutes blown this way are called *cross-blown* flutes. Our modern flute and its family are blown this way. People in many other countries build their flutes so that they may be sounded in this way.

There is another kind of cross-blown flute that is used in many parts of the world. The ancient Greeks called it a *syrinx* (SEER-rinks), or *pipes of Pan*.

The Greeks have a story of how the syrinx first came to be. The god of the forest, Pan, fell in love with a wood nymph named Syrinx. Frightened of this odd looking creature, she ran from him. He followed her. Suddenly she could run no farther because there was a river in the way. She prayed to the king of the gods, Zeus, to rescue her. Zeus saved her by turning her into a reed—a hollow plant that grows beside a river. Brokenhearted, Pan made a flute or syrinx out of the reed.

A syrinx is a group of hollow reeds of different lengths which have been bound together. Each reed is closed at the bottom. A player blows across the top of a reed to make a sound. Each reed can be used to make only one note. The longer reeds make lower sounds—the shorter reeds make higher sounds.

You see flutes that are blown the second way almost every day. Did you know that a whistle is a kind of flute? People in many countries have *whistle flutes*—flutes that are blown from the end.

Many such flutes have no finger-holes. Most, however, have finger-holes to change the notes. Many stores sell inexpensive wooden flutes with six holes for the fingers. A flute with six holes

11

is the same as seven whistles! As each hole is covered, the whistle becomes longer. Like the reeds of the syrinx, a longer whistle makes lower sounds. This picture shows how a six-holed flute is the same as seven whistles.

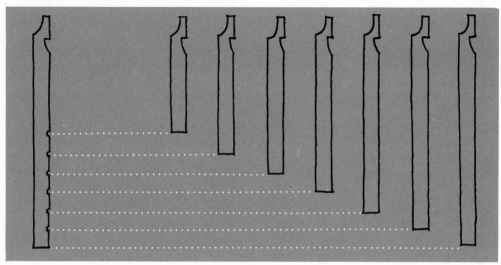

With just these six holes, you can play over fifteen notes! Here is how to play the first seven.

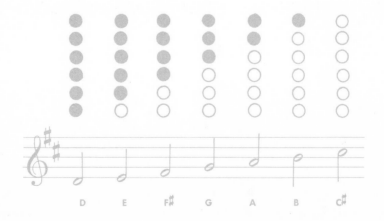

This sign (●), means that a hole is covered. This sign (○), means that a hole is not covered.

You can see that for the highest of the seven notes shown , all the holes are left uncovered. We can go much higher than this note. The next highest note is produced by putting all six fingers down again. The player blows a little harder to get this higher note. This is called *overblowing*. If the player continues overblowing, he can get all these notes.

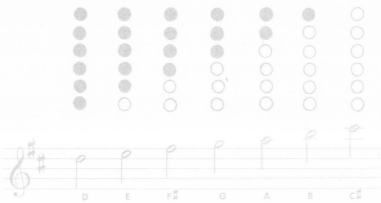

By using these fingerings, a player can go even higher.

All woodwind instruments use overblowing. If it were not for overblowing, it would not be possible to play nearly so many notes on a woodwind instrument.

Using the fingerings shown, can you figure out how this piece of music would be played?

Mary Had a Little Lamb

In order to give each note he plays a very clear beginning, a player of any wind instrument uses *tonguing*. This means that he starts each note by making a "t" sound with his tongue. The first two measures of *Mary Had a Little Lamb* would be *tongued* this way.

Sometimes, notes are connected with curved lines (⌣), called *slurs*. A wind player tongues only the first note in a group of notes which have been *slurred* together. If we put slurs into the first two measures of *Mary Had a Little Lamb*, it would be tongued this way.

14

Whistle flutes were used for many years. In Europe, they developed into a family of instruments called *recorders.* There are five sizes of recorders. The smallest is about 9½ inches long, while the longest is over 40 inches long.

The French call a recorder a *flûte á bec* — "a flute with a beak" — because the mouthpiece looks like the bill of a bird.

Besides having seven instead of six holes on the front, recorders have another hole on the back for the left thumb. When a player begins to overblow, he uncovers this hole a little—or *half-holes* it. This helps him to get the higher note more easily.

Recorders were used in orchestras until the time of Bach (1685-1750). Recorders began to be replaced in orchestras about Bach's time, because they are so difficult to play in tune. If a player blows a recorder loudly, the notes go *sharp,* or too high. If a player blows a recorder softly, the notes go *flat,* or too low. There is no way to control out-of-tune notes on the recorder except by using very special fingerings.

The recorder was replaced by the *transverse* flute. A transverse flute is one that is held "across" the player's face, like a modern flute. It is a cross-blown flute. The first transverse flutes did not look much like our modern flute. One of these early transverse flutes looked like a simple hollow tube with a blowhole and six finger-holes. The player of a transverse flute, however, could better control out-of-tune notes with his lips and his breath.

As time went on, keys were added to the flute, making the fingering much simpler. Even with these keys, the flute was still a very out-of-tune instrument. This is shown in a story about an orchestra conductor who had one flute in his orchestra. He complained to Cherubini, the composer, "What could be worse than having only one flute in an orchestra?" "Having two flutes!" replied Cherubini. If one flute couldn't stay in tune with itself, two flutes certainly couldn't stay in tune with each other.

We owe our modern flute to Theobald Boehm (BAY-em), a German who lived from 1794 to 1881. Boehm was a flute soloist who gave concerts all over Europe. He knew that the instrument he was playing was far from perfect. For one thing, the finger-holes were too close together to give the exactly correct notes. Finger-holes had to be placed this way because no flutist had large enough hands to cover correctly-placed holes. Also, the sound of the flute was not loud enough, mainly because the finger-holes were quite small. Again, this was because no flutist had large enough finger tips to cover holes of the right size.

Boehm took two flutes of the same length. Each flute had just a blowhole and no finger-holes. He cut off the end of the first flute until it gave the next higher note of the scale. After carefully measuring the length of the first flute, he bored a hole at the correct spot in the second flute. Then he cut more off the ·end of the first flute until he reached the next note of the scale. Again, after careful measurements, he bored a hole at the correct spot in the second flute.

He did this until he had bored the thirteen holes he needed. Then he had to invent a method for opening and closing these holes. Boehm fitted his new flute with keys to cover the holes. Certain keys were attached to other keys so that if a flutist presses one key, he also closes another. Boehm's first new flute model was completed in 1832. He continued working on improvements until his final model in 1847. This model is almost exactly the same as the flute that is played today.

Other Flutes

There are other members in our flute family. One that almost everybody knows is the *piccolo.* The full Italian name for the piccolo is *flauto piccolo,* which means "little flute".

The piccolo is a little less than half as long as a flute. Today, most piccolos are made of metal, although many are still being made of wood.

The piccolo can play all the notes from ♭ to ♭ .

The notes, however, that

come out sound an octave (eight notes)

higher. Therefore, we hear all the notes from ♭ to ♭ on the piccolo. The piccolo plays higher than any other orchestra or band instrument. Its clear, shrill tone makes it possible for this smallest of all instruments to be heard above all the other instruments in a large group.

Every good flutist also owns a piccolo. He can switch from playing the flute to playing the piccolo when the music in a band or orchestra requires it. He can do this quite easily, because all the notes on the piccolo are fingered exactly as they are on the flute.

There is another member of the flute family which very few people have seen, but which almost all of us have heard many, many times. It is the *alto flute.*

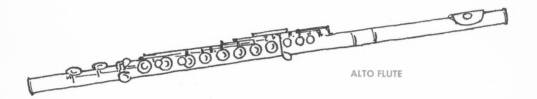

ALTO FLUTE

The alto flute looks like a very large flute. On it, a player plays

exactly the same notes as a regular flute—from ... to ...

—using exactly the same fingerings. The notes that we hear, how-

ever, are four notes lower—from ... to ... .

The alto flute was developed by Boehm and became his favorite instrument. Today, composers are writing more and more music that includes this beautiful instrument.

You may be surprised to learn that you can hear an alto flute almost every night of the week. It is used a great deal for television background music. Listen for it. You can recognize it because it can play lower notes much louder than a regular flute. It has a full, mellow tone. It can also play four notes lower than a regular flute.

There is one more member of the flute family. It is the *bass flute.* Like the alto flute, it plays the same notes as the regular flute. The notes that come out, however, are a full octave (eight

notes) lower—from   to   .

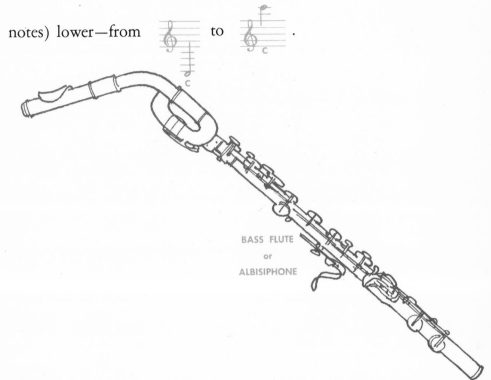

BASS FLUTE
or
ALBISIPHONE

The first bass flutes looked like huge, regular flutes. This type of flute was very clumsy to play. In 1910, an Italian, Abelardo Albisi, developed a new type of bass flute which is called the *albisiphone.* The body of the albisiphone is bent down toward the floor so the player may reach the keys more easily.

There are very few bass flutes, because there is very little music that has been written for it. Perhaps this instrument will become more popular some day.

ENGLISH HORN

20

The Oboe Family

What instrument makes us think of the "mysterious East", of India, Persia, Arabia, and of snake charmers? The oboe, of course. Why is this so? This is because the oboe came to us from the East, and because its ancestors are still being played there.

The oboe is a *double reed* instrument. This means that the reed is made of two pieces of cane. The best cane is grown in southern France. After it is cut, it is cured for three years. This means that it is stored first in the shade and then in the sun. After this curing process, it is ready to be made into reeds.

The two pieces of cane for an oboe reed are tied tightly to a metal tube with silk thread. The cane is then scraped to the proper shape. The lower part of the metal tube is covered with cork. This allows the reed to fit tightly into the top end of the oboe.

Most beginners on the oboe buy their reeds. More advanced players, however, like to make their own reeds. A finished oboe reed looks like this.

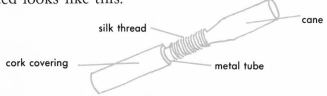

silk thread

cane

cork covering

metal tube

You can make a simple double reed instrument. Take a large drinking straw. Flatten one end for about ¾ of an inch. Trim the edges of the flattened part like this.

Now wet the end a little. Put this end a full 1½ inch into your mouth and blow quite hard. After a few tries, you should get a low buzz. Your breath makes the two free ends of the straw flutter together and apart very quickly. This causes the air in the straw to vibrate and to produce the note that you hear.

You can change this note by cutting two or three holes in the lower end of the straw and covering and uncovering them.

The earliest double reed instruments were made in exactly this way. The only difference was that men used the stems of hollow plants instead of drinking straws. These simple instruments were thrown away as soon as the reed wore out. A new instrument was quite simple to make.

As these early instruments developed, the reed was separated from the body of the instrument. If a reed wore out, then an entire instrument did not have to be thrown away and a new one made.

Double reed instruments were used mainly in the near-eastern countries. One such instrument was the *aulos*. The aulos was developed in ancient Greece. It was also used in ancient Egypt. In order to play it, most aulos players had to wear a leather band around their heads and across their cheeks. This was because the aulos used a very stiff, heavy reed, and the player had to blow very hard. The leather band helped him to keep up this strong pressure without hurting his cheeks.

22

Double reed instruments were brought to Europe from the East. By the fifteenth century, an entire family of instruments, called *shawms,* was developed. Shawms came in a number of sizes. The smallest was about 21 inches long — the longest was over 8 feet long.

SHAWM

About the middle of the seventeenth century, there appeared a new instrument — the oboe. The inside of the oboe was narrower than that of the shawm. The shawm was usually built in one piece. The oboe came in three parts — the *upper* joint, the *lower* joint, and the *bell* joint — besides the reed. The shawm had been used mostly for playing outdoor music. The newer oboe was used more for music played indoors. Soon, most orchestras had, besides the usual stringed instruments, a pair of flutes and a pair of the new oboes.

During the eighteenth century, except for the addition of a few keys, there were almost no improvements on this instrument. The oboe reached its present form during the nineteenth century. Most of the changes in the oboe were made by the Triebert family of Paris.

Do you remember how our modern flute was developed? Most of the work was done in a few years by one man. This is not true of the oboe. Our modern oboe took over 70 years to develop. The Triebert family worked on the oboe from 1810 to after 1880. They tried one change after another. They used many of Boehm's flute improvements on the oboe. They experimented with different kinds of wood, finally deciding that *grenadilla* wood was best. They also tried changing the shape of both the inside and the outside of the instrument. They experimented further with many, many new keys and fingerings. Most of these changes were not used in the final Triebert oboe model. This final model, except for a few, later additions, is the same as our present oboe.

Today, the oboe can play from   to   .

Like a flutist, an oboe player uses overblowing. To help him in overblowing, he uses a key in the back of the oboe, called the *octave key,* on all notes from   and higher. All woodwind instruments, except the flute and the bassoon, have some type of octave key to help the player to overblow.

Next time you see an oboe being played, notice the breathing of the player. Each time he stops to breathe, you will see him breathe *out* first, before he takes in fresh air. This is because the oboe uses very little air to produce a sound. Playing the oboe makes you feel somewhat like you do when you swim underwater. You must take a big gulp of air and hold it while you are swimming.

Like a flutist, an oboe player uses tonguing. Instead of making a "t" sound against the roof of his mouth, however, he touches the tip of the reed with his tongue.

24

The English Horn

You will often hear that "the English horn is neither English nor a horn". You can also read many stories of how this instrument might have received its name. The truth is, however, that no one is quite sure just why an English horn is called an English horn.

The English horn is a large oboe. When an oboe player plays the English horn, he uses exactly the same fingerings as on the oboe.

He can play from ♩ to ♩

The notes that come out are
five notes lower—from ♩ to ♩.

The reed of an English horn is tied to a metal tube like the oboe reed. The metal tube, however, is not covered with cork. The player slips the metal tube of the reed onto another metal tube, or *crook,* which is part of the instrument. The 4-inch crook is curved to make it easier for the player to reach the keys of this long instrument.

The end of the English horn — the *bell* — is rounded like a bulb. This, along with the narrow inside width of the instrument, somewhat softens and muffles the sound. Otherwise, the sound would be much louder and harsher.

The English horn is usually used to play smooth, slow, beautiful melodies.

BASSOON

CONTRABASSOON

(Not shown in proportion to bassoon)

The Bassoon Family

If you asked a group of people to decide which of all the instruments was the oddest looking, they would probably decide upon the bassoon. Sometimes you hear this instrument called the "clown of the orchestra". The bassoonist does not only play music that is meant to be amusing. He is often called upon to perform serious, beautiful music. There have even been fine concertos written for the bassoon.

What is a bassoon? Like the oboe, it is a double reed instrument. Of course, since the bassoon is so much larger than the oboe, its reed must also be larger. The two pieces of cane are bound together with wire and heavy thread. A bassoon reed looks like this. cane

thread← →wire

The reed fits onto the metal *crook,* or *bocal* (BOE-kul). The bocal is a curved metal tube, about 13½ inches long, that fits into the bassoon.

The bassoon itself is a tube that is 8 feet long. Because of its length, it is bent in two. The bassoon comes apart in five joints when it is ready to be put away. These joints are the *bocal,* the *wing* or *tenor* joint, the *double* or *butt* joint which contains the bend in the instrument, the *bass* or *long* joint, and the *bell* joint.

Here is how these five joints are put together.

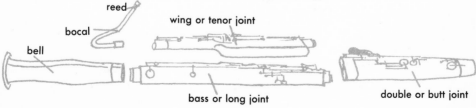

reed
bocal
wing or tenor joint
bell
bass or long joint
double or butt joint

In order to play a bassoon, a player needs to have rather large hands. This is why most bassoonists begin their study of music on another instrument such as the piano or the clarinet. Later, about junior high age, when their hands have grown, they start the study of the bassoon.

No player would have large enough hands to cover the finger-holes on a bassoon if the holes were bored straight into the instrument as they are on other woodwinds. The holes are bored at an angle. On the inside of the bassoon, the holes are where they belong in order to produce the correct notes. On the outside, however, the holes are close enough together so that they can be covered by the fingers of the player. Here is a cross section of how the bassoon finger-holes are bored.

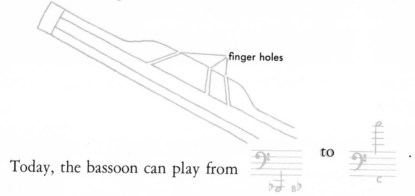

Today, the bassoon can play from ... to ...

Bassoons are usually made of maple wood, although some student models now are being made of *ebonite* — a hard, black rubber. Wooden bassoons usually have an ivory ring at the top of the bell joint.

Like the oboe, the bassoon is related to the shawm and another old instrument called the *curtal.* The bass shawms and curtals had to be doubled like a bassoon because they were so long.

The bassoon first appeared about 1650. By the eighteenth century, the bassoon had from four to eight keys.

During the nineteenth century, many people tried their luck at improving the fingering of the bassoon. Adolphe Sax, whom we will meet later, brought out a new bassoon model. The Triebert family tried to use some of Boehm's developments on the bassoons they made. Most of these "improvements" made the fingerings simpler, but they also made the tone of the instrument suffer.

We owe our modern bassoon to the Heckel family of Biebrich, Germany. They managed to improve the fingering of the bassoon without damaging the instrument's tone. Even today, many professional bassoonists play bassoons made by the Heckel Company.

The Contrabassoon

There is another size of bassoon called the *contrabassoon,* or *double-bassoon.* This instrument is twice as long as a bassoon. Therefore, it is folded four times. The bell of the contrabassoon points downward.

The contrabassoon can play most of the same notes as the bassoon — from to and uses the same fingerings. The notes that we hear, however, come out an octave (eight notes) lower.

The contrabassoon plays lower than any other band or orchestra instrument. In spite of its large size, though, it is a very soft instrument.

The Clarinet Family

Of all the woodwind instruments, the hardest to develop was the clarinet. Let's find out why.

The clarinet is a *single reed* instrument. This means that one piece of cane, which has been attached to the mouthpiece, is made to flutter back and forth by the player's breath. The fluttering reed causes the air in the instrument to vibrate and to make the sound that we hear.

Man has had single reed instruments for many centuries. They were even used in ancient Egypt. The reeds of these early instruments were usually part of the instrument. Later, reeds were made separately and were tied to the mouthpiece.

Single reed instruments were not used as much as double reeds. Still, musicians in most countries had some sort of single reed instrument to play. In Europe, the forerunner of the clarinet was the *chalumeau* (shall-uh-MOE). The chalumeau was a single reed instrument about nine inches long. It usually had seven holes — six holes on top for the fingers, and one hole for the left thumb.

The chalumeau was not used very much in early orchestras because it could only play eight notes — usually from [♪] to [♪] . Do you remember how the other woodwind instruments use overblowing? Remember our simple flute. With six fingers covering all the holes, we can play [♪] . With the same fingering, if we overblow, we can play [♪] . The overblown note is an octave (eight notes) higher than the first note. We say that this flute *overblows at the octave.*

The chalumeau does not overblow at the octave. There are two reasons for this. One reason is the type of mouthpiece and reed used. The other reason is the shape of the inside of the instrument. The inside of the chalumeau, and of our clarinet, is a *cylinder.* This means that the inside width is about the same at the top as it is near the bottom. Because of the mouthpiece and the inside of the instrument, the chalumeau *overblows at the twelfth.* This means that if the player overblows this note, [♪] , he gets this note [♪] . The second note is twelve notes higher than the first.

The notes a chalumeau can play are [♪] to [♪] . If the player used overblowing, he could also play [♪] to about [♪] . This means that the notes between [♪] and [♪] would be missing. You can see that writing music for this instrument would be almost impossible because notes were missing right out of the middle of its range. The short pieces of music written for the chalumeau, therefore, only used the eight notes from 🎵(G) to 🎵(G) .

The clarinet was invented about 1675 by Johann Christian Denner of Nuremburg, Germany. He made an instrument a little over twice as long as a chalumeau, and bored seven holes in it. It could play from 🎵(G) to 🎵(G) . Then he added an *octave* or *speaker* key to help the player to overblow. This made all these notes 🎵(G to G and D to B) possible. Denner's problem was how to produce the missing notes, 🎵(A B C) .

In the extra long bell joint, Denner bored another hole for 🎵(F) . He covered this hole with a key to be operated by the player's little finger. When this note 🎵(F) was overblown, the missing 🎵(C) was produced.

Denner made the still missing 🎵(A) and 🎵(B) possible by adding holes and keys near the top of the instrument, above the hole for 🎵(G) . Now all the notes from 🎵(F) to about 🎵(B) were possible. Later, someone added another key for 🎵(E) at the bottom of the clarinet. This made it much easier to overblow the 🎵(B) .

During the eighteenth century, composers began writing music for the clarinet. It was also used more and more in orchestras. Instrument makers began to add keys to make the clarinet's fingering easier and to make the instrument play better in tune.

The earliest clarinets were played with the mouthpiece turned so that the reed was uppermost. German players soon discovered that they could more easily control the tone and intonation (in-tune-ness) of the clarinet if they turned the mouthpiece around so the reed was on the bottom. This custom soon spread into all other countries. At first, the reed was tied to the mouthpiece by wrapping it round and round with heavy string. Today, however, most clarinets use a metal *ligature* to attach the reed.

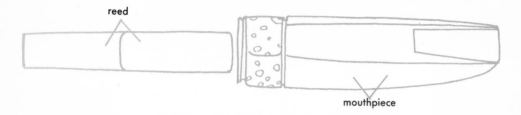

reed

mouthpiece

The clarinet reached its present form during the nineteenth century. The clarinet that is used most today is the *Boehm-system* clarinet. Surprisingly enough, Boehm never did any work on the clarinet.

Our modern clarinet was developed in 1843, by a professor of clarinet at the Paris Conservatory, Hyacinthe Klosé. He called his clarinet fingering system the Boehm-system because most of the improvements he used were borrowed from Boehm's new flute model. Klosé's clarinet model is almost the same as the clarinet we use today.

34

A clarinet has five joints — the *mouthpiece,* the *barrel,* the *upper* joint, the *lower* joint, and the *bell.*

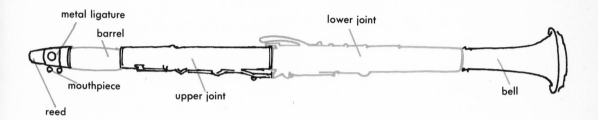

metal ligature

barrel

lower joint

mouthpiece

upper joint

bell

reed

Fine clarinets are made of *grenadilla* wood, a type of ebony. This type of wood is grown in South Africa. It is a very hard, heavy wood that is dark brown and purple when it is cut. After it has been dried and aged for five to ten years, it is even darker. Before this wood is used to make an instrument, it is soaked with oil, which turns it black.

Mouthpieces have been made of ebony, ivory, plastic, and even crystal. Most, however, are now made of *ebonite,* a very hard, black rubber. Many, less expensive clarinets are also made of ebonite.

Today, the clarinet family is quite a large one. Clarinets come in many different sizes, or keys. All clarinets, however, play exactly the same notes—from to —and use exactly the same fingerings. The notes that come out, of course, are different, and depend on the type of clarinet.

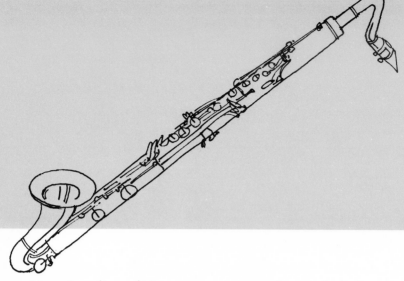

Here is a list of the more commonly used clarinets, and of the notes we hear them play.

The *E♭ Clarinet*—This is the smallest of the clarinets. It has a very shrill tone. It plays from to .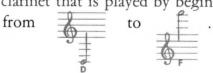

The *B♭ Clarinet*—This is the most common clarinet, and the clarinet that is played by beginners. It plays from to .

The *A Clarinet*—Most good clarinet players also own an A clarinet. Some music is easier to play on the A clarinet than on the B♭ clarinet. The A clarinet also has a fuller, richer tone than the B♭ clarinet. It plays from to

36

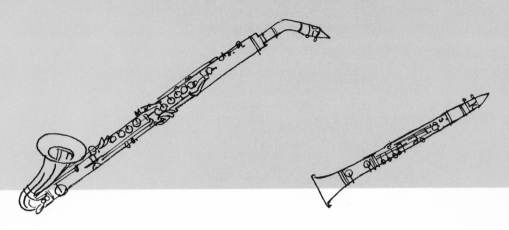

The *E♭ Alto Clarinet*—This is an alto clarinet that is used more in bands than in orchestras. It plays from [music notation: G, bass clef] to [music notation: B♭, treble clef].

The *B♭ Bass Clarinet*—The deep, full tone of this instrument adds much to any group in which it is used. It plays from [music notation: D, bass clef] to [music notation: F, treble clef].

The *BB♭ Contra-Bass Clarinet*—This large instrument is used mostly in bands. It plays from [music notation: bass clef] to [music notation: D, bass clef] [music notation: F, bass clef].

The alto, bass, and contra-bass clarinets all have curved barrels and bells because of their length. In addition, the contra-bass clarinet sometimes has an extra turn in the upper joint to make it easier to handle.

SOPRANO

ALTO

TENOR

BARITONE

The Saxophone Family

The saxophone is, perhaps, the best known of all the wood-wind instruments. We see it in almost every dance band. Some of the larger bands even use four or more saxophones. We even see the saxophone in many small "combos" of two or three musicians. Besides being used in large symphony bands, the saxophone is also used in symphony orchestras. There, we might not recognize it, because it is played with a beautiful, "straight" tone that is not often used for dance band work.

The saxophone was patented in 1846 by Adolphe Sax. Do you remember this Paris instrument maker from the section on the bassoon? No one knows just how he got the idea for this instrument. Perhaps the idea came when he tried to play a brass instrument with a clarinet mouthpiece.

The saxophone is the only woodwind instrument that has never been made of wood. Sax meant the saxophone as a link between the brass and woodwind instruments. It is made of brass, but it uses keys like a woodwind instrument. Its mouthpiece and reed are a great deal like those of a clarinet. Although the saxophone, like the clarinet, is played pointing towards the floor, the fingering system of the saxophone is almost exactly like that of the flute.

Saxophones usually have three parts—the *mouthpiece,* the *neck,* and the *body.*

The saxophone began to be used a little in orchestras during the second half of the nineteenth century. It was used even more in military bands. The biggest push for the popularity of this instrument, however, was given in the United States during the 1920's. During those years, jazz was catching on in this country. The saxophone was found to be the perfect instrument for this type of music.

Sax's first saxophone family had fourteen different sizes in it. Today there are seven members in the saxophone family. They all play the same notes—from to —and use the same fingerings. The notes that we hear, however, depend on the size of the saxophone that is being played. Here is a list of the five most-used saxophones and the notes that we hear.

The B♭ *Soprano Saxophone*—This is not a well-known member of the saxophone family. It is the only saxophone that usually comes without a curved shape. It plays from to .

The E♭ *Alto Saxophone*—This is the saxophone played by most beginners. It plays from to .

The B♭ *Tenor Saxophone*—This saxophone plays from to .

The E♭ *Baritone Saxophone*—This saxophone is so large, it has an extra curve in its neck. It plays from to .

The B♭ *Bass Saxophone*—This is the largest saxophone you will see. It plays from to .

40

The Woodwinds

This book has told the stories of the five woodwind families. You have discovered where they came from, how they work, and how they have developed into the instruments we know today.

The next time you hear a group of musicians perform—whether the group is a "combo" of only three members, a brilliant marching band, or a fine symphony orchestra — watch for and listen to the woodwind instruments. Knowing more about these instruments will help you to appreciate the woodwinds and their place in the world of music more than ever before. But even more important, we hope that knowing more about the woodwinds has made you want to learn to play one of them yourself.

ABOUT THE AUTHOR

Jean Craig is a native of Cleveland, Ohio. Her early musical training was at the Cleveland Music School Settlement, where she studied violin, piano, and music theory. She is a graduate of the Oberlin Conservatory of Music, with a degree in music education. For the past four years, Miss Craig has taught music in the Cedar Rapids, Iowa public schools. She also plays in the Cedar Rapids Symphony Orchestra and teaches violin and flute privately. Currently she is enrolled as a graduate student in music and music education at Teachers College, Columbia University.

NOTEWORTHY BOOKS

MUSICAL BOOKS FOR YOUNG PEOPLE

THE ALPHABET OF MUSIC
THE BEAT OF THE DRUM
FOLK INSTRUMENTS
FOLLOW THE LEADER [Story of Conducting]
THE HEART OF THE ORCHESTRA [Story of Strings]
KEYBOARD INSTRUMENTS
PLACES OF MUSICAL FAME
PLAYBACK: THE STORY OF RECORDING DEVICES
SHINING BRASS [Story of Trumpet and Brass]
THE STORY OF MUSICAL NOTES
THE STORY OF MUSICAL ORGANIZATIONS
THE WOODWINDS

MEDICAL BOOKS FOR CHILDREN AND YOUNG PEOPLE

DEAR LITTLE MUMPS CHILD
DENTISTS' TOOLS
DOCTORS' TOOLS
FUR, FEATHERS, HAIR
HOW WE HEAR [Story of Hearing]
KAREN GETS A FEVER
LEFTY [Story of Left-Handedness]
MICHAEL GETS THE MEASLES
PENNY THE MEDICINE MAKER [Story of Penicillin]
PETER GETS THE CHICKENPOX
RED MAN, WHITE MAN, AFRICAN CHIEF
    [Story of Skin Color]
THEY WOULDN'T QUIT [Story of Handicapped]
TWINS [Story of Twins]
WHY GLASSES? [Story of Vision]

The above books are written by competent authorities and attractively illustrated. Information about obtaining these is available from

Lerner Publications Company

133 FIRST AVENUE NORTH
MINNEAPOLIS 1, MINNESOTA